Nina Millns

Service

Salamander Street

PLAYS

First published in 2022 by Salamander Street Ltd.
(info@salamanderstreet.com)

Service © Nina Millns, 2022

ISBN: 9781914228667

10 9 8 7 6 5 4 3 2 1

*Dedicated to the memory of my yiayia, Ourania Economidou,
and my pappou, the original Andreas Economides.*

And to all those affected by the Windrush Scandal.

Characters

DIMITRI, late 30s / 40, originally from Cyprus

FITZ, 82, black, Caribbean (hardly any trace of accent)

MANNY, British born South Asian

OFFICER, white, English

Act One

SCENE ONE

2018.

A comfortable room with two chairs facing each other. A small side-table next to one of the chairs. A box of tissues and a small clock facing the other chair on the table. Perhaps a plant or a serene work of art framed on the wall. A door upstage.

Voices from O.S. The door opens and **MANNY** *leads* **DIMITRI** *into the room.*

MANNY: I've put you in here for the duration. Nice and contained but with easy access to the emergency exit. They're all fully accessible so that shouldn't be a problem. Complimentary tissues. Happy with that?

DIMITRI: It's great, thank you.

MANNY: Good. I've ensured the same room will be available each time. Consistency is important.

DIMITRI: Yes.

MANNY: Speaking of… We've got Thursdays in for supervision. Is that still convenient?

DIMITRI: Yes, Thursdays would be great.

MANNY: Ok. I'll confirm that too. So we're starting you off on Wednesday with your first client. That's this week and – all being well – for the five weeks following. And we'll build up your hours as we go along.

DIMITRI: Right.

MANNY: Now. The forms. *(He holds out a clipboard with several copies of the same form attached. He hands it to* **DIMITRI**.*)* I'm sure you've been briefed but I will just take the liberty of reiterating how important it is to get these bad boys filled in right. We need a nice, clear, fully completed form at the end of each session, so make sure you allow extra time for that.

DIMITRI: Yes, of course.

MANNY: If you need more copies, you've got plenty there, but there's more where they came from so do ask.

DIMITRI: Thank you.

MANNY: And I've also attached a pen to the top there. But if you need more, if it's not working… do ask.

DIMITRI: Great.

MANNY: Any time.

Pause.

I'm here most hours the centre's open so I'm usually to hand. Apart from Tuesday nights.

DIMITRI: Right.

MANNY: Band rehearsals.

DIMITRI: Oh right.

MANNY: I'm in a band. Bass. Yeah. We've actually got a few gigs lined up, so.

DIMITRI: That's great.

Pause.

So Wednesday… You'll be here if… when… if I need…

MANNY: Wednesdays are clear. So yes I'll make sure you're set up ok beforehand. But don't worry, we're not in the habit of pushing our trainees in at the deep end. We're starting you off nice and gently. *(He checks his notes.)* Yes. An elderly man I believe. Eighties. So should be pretty straightforward. Ease you in so to speak.

DIMITRI: Great.

MANNY: Great.

SCENE TWO

FITZ: *(Angry, shaken.)* I didn't see them coming, did I. They ambushed me.

DIMITRI *nods.*

FITZ: Three on one. How's that a fair fight?

DIMITRI: I'm so sorry.

FITZ: Bloody cowards. Don't have the guts to fight me man to man. I'd slay them. Annihilate the lot of them.

DIMITRI: It must have been terrifying.

FITZ: Nah. Nah. I've seen much worse. Much worse. I ain't scared. Take a lot more'n that to scare me. Just fight me proper, you know?

DIMITRI: Ok.

FITZ: It's gotta be a fair fight. Otherwise… I used to be in the army.

DIMITRI: Yes, it says here. How long were you –

FITZ: I'll bring you a photo next time. You shoulda seen me. I was a machine, son. A machine. They would have pissed their pants just looking at me. Just one look and they would have scarpered.

DIMITRI: It must be difficult not to have the strength you used to have.

FITZ: What you talking about? They ambushed me! It wasn't a fair fight. I would've… I would've… Back in the day I would've…

DIMITRI: Is that why you wanted to come and talk? Was it the mugging that made you want to come?

FITZ: You shoulda seen me…

DIMITRI: That level of violence can be very traumatic…

FITZ: There's no respect. Where's the respect? You got to respect your elders. I'm a veteran for god's sake. They got me holed up in that stinking flat. Months I've been calling them to fix the heating. They don't care about me. Living like a bloody… Where's the respect?

DIMITRI: That sounds really tough.

Pause.

FITZ: Months I've been calling. I even went down there. I get a different one every time. Don't know who I am. Don't care... I've told them the same thing ten times to ten different people. They don't give a damn. Looking at me like I'm a useless old... I'm a veteran.

DIMITRI: It is very important that you're allowed to live with dignity.

FITZ: Just a bit of respect. A bit of dignity...

Pause.

DIMITRI: Is there anything else that has been troubling you? Anything else you want to talk about?

FITZ: And I told them about those stairs too. They congregate there. Smash the lights so you've got to climb up in the dark. And then they attack.

DIMITRI: It says down at the bottom here "Flashbacks".

FITZ: I told them to fix it. They got to put cameras up or something. Sort it out.

DIMITRI: Would you like to explain what you meant when you wrote down Flashbacks?

FITZ: I don't use the lifts. Don't need to. I'm fit as a fiddle, me. Eighty-two years old son.

DIMITRI: When do the flashbacks happen?

FITZ: I leap up them stairs like a twenny-year-old.

DIMITRI: Are they frequent?

FITZ: Like a twenny-year-old.

Pause.

DIMITRI: Fitzroy?

Pause.

FITZ: It's Fitz.

DIMITRI: Fitz.

Pause.

FITZ: They stink of piss anyway.

DIMITRI *looks confused.*

The lifts.

DIMITRI *nods.*

Pause.

They stink.

Pause.

Where are you…. What about… You ever been in the army?

DIMITRI: Would you like to tell me about it? What it was like?

FITZ: It's a job. Innit. You got a job. It's a job. You do the job, son. Don't ask why or how. You take your orders and you do the job.

Pause.

Discipline. That's what you learn. Discipline. That's what's missing nowadays. A good bit of discipline. And some respect.

Pause.

I wasn't even meant to be out that late. They messed up my pension didn't they? Stupid… I had to go all the way to the council. Sat there for an hour and a half.

Pause.

I had to go three weeks without my pension. I'm a decorated veteran. I'll bring my medals next time. For bravery. Service to the… It was dark when I came out. Stupid idiots. No discipline. No organisation. Sitting behind that desk like a bloody… useless… Looking at me like I was some useless old fart. I wanted to clobber him upside his face. *Don't you gawp at me, son. You wouldn't have a pot to piss in if it wasn't for the likes of me…* It took them ages to fix it. And then it was dark and those stupid stairs…

DIMITRI: That's really tough, Fitz. Three weeks with no pension.

FITZ: Ha! That's nothing, son. Three weeks? I'm a survivor. You could chuck me anywhere in the world and I'd have a fire going and a flag flying in no time. No time.

Pause.

This city life you're living – it's no good son. You got to know how to survive Out There. In the elements.

DIMITRI: You must have had to survive in some pretty extreme situations.

FITZ: What would you know about that?

DIMITRI: *(Carefully.)* …I'm sure I would have found it very hard. I'm sure I would have felt very scared. Very alone.

Pause.

FITZ: Ha!... You ever…? Where you from anyway? What's your… your… background?

DIMITRI: Would it be helpful for you to know a bit more about me? It must seem quite strange talking to someone about all this when you don't know very much about me.

FITZ: Oh I've met all sorts, son. All sorts. All over the world. You name it. I been all over. When I was serving. Seen it all. Made friends. Made enemies. All sorts. Oh the stories I could tell you. I've lived several lifetimes in one. That's me.

DIMITRI: That's pretty incredible Fitz. I hope I get to hear about some of it.

FITZ: *(Looking carefully at* **DIMITRI***. Then,)* Nah. You don't want to hear about all that. Just an old man talking about a bunch of dead people. They're long gone all them lot. Long gone… I'm probably the last one standing…

Pause.

DIMITRI: We're coming to the end of the session, Fitz. We've got a few minutes left and I wanted to check how you're doing?

FITZ: I'm fine.

DIMITRI: Ok.

Pause.

Well, there's a form we need to fill in before you go. Would you like to...?

DIMITRI *hands over the form.* **FITZ** *glances at it but doesn't take it.*

FITZ: I ain't got my glasses.

DIMITRI: There's a version with larger font if it's easier...

FITZ: I thought we were talking, not reading.

DIMITRI: Well, yes, but we just have to go through this –

FITZ: You'll have to read it for me.

DIMITRI: Ok. Well... Er... "At the end of this session would you say your anxiety levels are a) lower than before, b) the same, or c) worse?"

FITZ: My what?

DIMITRI: Your anxiety levels.

FITZ: I haven't got anxiety.

DIMITRI: Ok. So. I'll just put b) the same. So, in terms of feelings of depression would you say after the session you feel a) less depressed, b) the same, c) more depressed?

FITZ: What? I'm not – What's all this – ?

DIMITRI: It's just some routine questions I have to –

FITZ: What else does it say?

DIMITRI: Well the next one... Let's see... "Over the last two weeks, how often have you felt tired or that you have little or no energy...?

FITZ: I'm eighty-fucking-two!

DIMITRI: Ok... So... "Frequently"...

DIMITRI *looks up at* **FITZ** *and puts the form down.*

Perhaps just for this week we can leave it there.

FITZ: Are we done?

DIMITRI: For this week.

> **FITZ** *struggles to his feet and walks slowly to the door.*

> **DIMITRI** *stands too.*

> **FITZ** *pauses at the door.*

FITZ: Every night. They happen every night.

> **FITZ** *opens the door and hobbles out.*

SCENE THREE

DIMITRI: He was shaking. Physically shaking…

MANNY: With rage?

DIMITRI: He was terrified. It was… I wanted to…

MANNY: …To… What?

DIMITRI: I had this urge to make myself smaller. I found myself sitting in a way… I was trying to show him… There wasn't any threat. It was safe. I was safe. I didn't know how.

I suddenly became very aware of how much space I take up. In a room. I hadn't been sized up like that for… Every word was a challenge. I dare you. I fucking dare you…

MANNY: I dare you to… Fight me?

DIMITRI: Let me down. I dare you to be like all the others. Go on. Show me I'm right. Prove me right. Again.

I was The System. I was the doctor that made him wait. The council that kept him cold. The pension that didn't come. I was the ten different people he had to tell the same story to. Who looked at him like he was just another case number. I was yet another person he had to start again with. And he was angry. But he was also terrified. And I just wanted to…

MANNY: Why? Why did you want to…?

DIMITRI: Well… I know fear. I know being let down. Having to be tough. Having to man up.

Pause.

MANNY: What else.

DIMITRI: I wanted to show respect. I wanted to give him the respect he deserves. It made me think of my own. My grandfather. I wanted to… To treat him the way I wished my grandfather was… I wanted him to feel the dignity his service, his age, he deserved…

MANNY: What else.

DIMITRI: I wanted to.. show… I'm not like them. I'm not the doctor and the council and.

MANNY: What are you?

DIMITRI: Well. I'm his counsellor. But…

MANNY: But?

DIMITRI: But we're also two people in a room trying to talk about stuff. Stuff that's really…

I'm not them. I'm not going to make him wait. I'm not going to make him repeat himself ten times. I'm not…

MANNY: You're not…?

DIMITRI: I'm not… The System. I'm not the system.

Pause.

MANNY: And yet. You are also part of… Working within… Answerable to a –

DIMITRI: Well, if we're going to get existential –

MANNY: – practical –

DIMITRI: – about it –

MANNY: – realistic.

Pause.

Why does it feel hard to identify with a…

DIMITRI: Well, it's not… human. It doesn't allow for… two… people trying to… to… Isn't that the core of what we do here?

MANNY: What did you suggest in terms of strategies? [To cope with the fallout from the attack?]

DIMITRI: Well, it's a bit more complicated. It's not just the mugging. He put down flashbacks.

MANNY: Since the mugging?

DIMITRI: I don't think so.

MANNY: Ok. Let's be realistic.

DIMITRI: He's an eighty-year-old army veteran. He –

MANNY: You've got six sessions, Dimitri. Six. That's it.

DIMITRI: He wrote it down.

MANNY: Five left.

DIMITRI: He's asking for help.

MANNY: He's come for help to deal with the recent incident –

DIMITRI: It's not just that. He wrote down Flashbacks –

MANNY: You have a professional duty to ensure that he doesn't leave feeling worse than –

DIMITRI: It's taken him decades, Manny. Decades to walk through that door and –

MANNY: It's been a few weeks since the attack –

DIMITRI: He wants to process all those years of –

MANNY: You've got six sessions.

DIMITRI: So, what. I'm just meant to ignore it? Is that what we do?

MANNY: What we do is focus on what we can help them with in the time allocated so that we don't leave them worse off –

DIMITRI: So that the forms look better off –

MANNY: Ok. Dimitri. You are a gifted practitioner.

DIMITRI: Look, I don't need –

MANNY: No, no it's important. Your instinct is right. It's spot on. And you have heart and humanity and the skills to really help. And. One of the things these hours are about is getting a realistic sense of what it is that you can actually help with.

DIMITRI: Within the limits of…

MANNY: Within the limits.

DIMITRI: Of?

MANNY: Well, within the time limits…

DIMITRI: And..?

MANNY: Within your limits.

DIMITRI: What else.

MANNY: As a professional who is still learning –

DIMITRI: – What else.

MANNY: Within the limited sessions…

DIMITRI: Within the limits of…?

MANNY: Within the limits of –

DIMITRI: The System.

MANNY: Yes. The system.

Pause.

It's just a set of boundaries. Limits: Boundaries.

DIMITRI: Limitations: Failings.

MANNY: You're not failing anyone Dimitri. You can't carry his entire history of PTSD on your shoulders. That's not boundaried. What you *can* do is help him learn some techniques to process what just happened, seeing as it shook him up.

DIMITRI: He doesn't sleep properly.

MANNY: Great. So. There are a number of mindfulness techniques you can show him to help with that. What else?

DIMITRI: He can't read.

MANNY: So you can help him plan a trip to the opticians.

DIMITRI: I don't think he can read.

MANNY: Ok. Let's keep this contained.

DIMITRI: He couldn't even fill out the form –

MANNY: Enough. You are not going to teach him to read. You are not going to solve or even touch his flashbacks and you are not going to fuck up my forms. What you *are* going to do is suggest some very effective mindfulness techniques, offer some CBT and bring me back six completed forms with a lovely arc that ends in a nice low number. Is that clear?

DIMITRI: And what about –

MANNY: I'm sorry but –

DIMITRI: He's come to us for –

MANNY: Is. That. Clear.

SCENE FOUR

FITZ *is holding a box he has opened.*

FITZ: I forgot this was in here… That's my wallet. Standard issue leather wallet. It's still got a rollie from back then. Jesus… That's over fifty years old that baccy. That'd give you a kick, wouldn't it. I'd give it a go, light it up, except I gave all that up a long time ago now. On account of my… well… everything really. Some old money… Can't use any of that now. Look at that *(He hands* **DIMITRI** *a photo.)* Who d'you reckon that is then? Three guesses.

DIMITRI: *(Smiles.)* It's you.

FITZ: Got it in one. *(Chuckles.)* Haven't changed that much then. Look at that, look at that. I was a machine son. Invincible. Look at those arms. You wouldn't want to get on the wrong side o' them would you? *(He holds up his arms.)* I haven't lost it, you know. You never do. Look at that. Not bad for an old codger, eh?...I was a tank...

And this. Guess who that's from.

FITZ *hands* **DIMITRI** *an envelope with a letter in it.* **DIMITRI** *opens it carefully.*

That's from my mate Liz. Up in Buckingham. To say thank you for my service. Services to the... Me old mucker Liz...

He replaces it all carefully.

DIMITRI: That's a pretty remarkable treasure trove there Fitz. There are some valuable things in there.

FITZ: ...Me old pal Liz... Me old mucker...HRH...

DIMITRI: Thank you for showing me.

FITZ: *(Lifting his arm.)* Look at that. Go on. Touch it.

DIMITRI: I can see from here.

FITZ: Hard as bricks. Still got it.

DIMITRI: Very impressive.

FITZ: A fucking tank I was... Come on. I'll wrestle ya. Go on. I dare ya. Come on.

DIMITRI: ... I don' think –

FITZ: I'll do it with me left hand. I don't care. You arty types. You're all left-handed i'nt ya? Go on. I dare you.

DIMITRI: I'm not going to wrestle you, Fitz.

FITZ: I'm only joking. Look at the face on you. Relax, I'm only pulling your leg.

I was a machine, son. I was…

DIMITRI: You were very strong, Fitz. You must have taken great pride in your fitness. Your health.

FITZ: That's discipline, son. Right there. You don't look like that sitting on your backside all day listening to other people's problems. That's up at dawn, doing ten miles before breakfast and ten more if you're slacking. That's push-ups and sit-ups 'til you throw-up. That's ask no questions, take your orders, keep your head down, nose clean and arse wiped. That's elbow grease and boot polish and good old-fashioned sweat, son. That's discipline.

There's none o' that now. No discipline. No respect…

DIMITRI: It must be hard to see how people's values have changed.

FITZ: You used to respect your elders. There was a hierarchy. A chain of command. You wouldn't hear of anyone disrespecting an old man like that. A veteran… I've seen things… I've… I've… I've been to hell and back… I've…

DIMITRI: This recent attack. I've been wondering if you wanted to try some techniques that might help you process what happened.

FITZ: What happened? When?

DIMITRI: The attack.

FITZ: Yeah. Yeah. The attack. I still remember it… I still… Every night I…

DIMITRI: …Well it was only a few weeks ago so it would still be fresh in your mind. And since it happened so close to home, it must have been even more upsetting.

FITZ: Home? No… No… I wasn't at home… I was –

DIMITRI: You were on the stairs, outside your flat.

FITZ: My flat? Oh that? You mean… I thought you meant…

DIMITRI: You came to talk about the recent mugging on the stairs near your flat.

Pause.

FITZ: Yeah.

DIMITRI: So, what we can do is perhaps start with a bit of mindful breathing.

FITZ: Eh?

DIMITRI: It's just a way of keeping us in the present. Reminding us that right now we are safe. We are here, now.

FITZ: What you on about?

DIMITRI: Shall we –? Let's give it a go. Why don't you put the box down and just sit with your feet on the ground.

FITZ: Where else would they be?

DIMITRI: And if it feels right you can close your eyes… Otherwise you can keep them open… But the main thing is that you focus on the area just outside your nostrils where the air goes in… And then out… In… And out…

And if it feels right, to say, I have a body, but I am not my body… I have thoughts, and I am not my thoughts. I have feelings and I am more than my feelings… Or you can think it, silently. In your head… Whatever feels right…

Pause.

Was that… Did you… How did you find doing that?

FITZ: Yeah. No. It was. Different, like.

DIMITRI: I've found that finding ways to keep myself in the here and now really lowers my anxiety.

FITZ: Yeah.

DIMITRI: It might help with the stress of the last few weeks.

Pause.

FITZ: I thought you… You kept going on about… That form. The one I had to bring in.

DIMITRI: What about the form?

FITZ: That bit. At the bottom. You kept going on about it –

DIMITRI: I'm sorry if you felt I was pushing you to talk about things you didn't –

FITZ: Don't you want to talk about it then?

DIMITRI: About what?

FITZ: About… The thing I said… At the… At the end…

DIMITRI: Would you like to talk about it?

FITZ: You were the one going on about it. Made me tell you… It's your job, isn't it? Where you…? That name, what is it, Russian? Eastern Europe? What?

DIMITRI: Why do you think it would it be helpful for you to know where my name is from?

FITZ: We had all sorts in our squad. All sorts. We had a Kiwi for a bit. He was alright. An Indian fella. Or Gurkha or something. Couple of Irish lads, like. But I was the only black fella.

We went all over, we did. I bet I been more places in the world than you been on holidays. I passed through India an' all. Before you learned your breathing in the nostrils malarkey. They were doing all that fifty years ago. More. That breathing malarkey. Tell you what though. They were bloody ruthless fighters, they were. Ruthless. All that breathing, sitting still for hours. And then Pow! They've sliced your head off with a machete before you can say chai and two sugars.

DIMITRI: How long were you stationed in India?

FITZ: Ah no, just passing through, like. I was all over the Middle East though. Saudi Arabia, Oman, Afghanistan right at the start of it all. Falklands… Mostly six months here. Six months there. And then two years straight on a little island. Tiny place called Cyprus. Paradise it was. And hell. A living hell. Hot as hell too. Savage hot. Each place they sent me was hotter than the next. Filthy fighters, them lot. Outright terrorists. That's when… That's why… Why I got my letter. From the Queen. For my services to the…

DIMITRI: Yes the letter. Thank you for showing me that, Fitz. That was really interesting to see all those… those… So… We're coming to the end now.

FITZ: Already? That went by quick.

DIMITRI: Yes. It did… So I just have to… the form. Do you… do you have your glasses or…?

FITZ: No glasses.

DIMITRI: Ok… So shall I just… How are you feeling? In general, at the end of this time together?

FITZ: Whatever you put down last time, put down a bit better this time.

DIMITRI: Ok… Well, for example where it says –

FITZ: Put down one better. Apart from the bit about being tired. I'm still bleeding tired. I'm still eighty-two.

DIMITRI: Ok… So… I'll just put… Ok, great. Thank you Fitz.

FITZ: We done?

DIMITRI: Yes.

FITZ: *(Getting up.)* Same time next week?

DIMITRI: Sure.

SCENE FIVE

MANNY: Ok. Well let's just take a moment.

DIMITRI: I have.

MANNY: Let's take another one and just…

DIMITRI: I've thought it through.

MANNY: It's been a few hours, Dimitri. I think you could benefit from a bit more –

DIMITRI: I wanted to give you as much time as possible to find –

MANNY: Why don't we put any decisions aside for now and just talk?

DIMITRI *nods.*

It's really affected you. This disclosure. What in particular was difficult about it?

DIMITRI: He was stationed in Cyprus.

MANNY: And?

DIMITRI: And I'm from Cyprus.

Pause.

That's it. There's no subtext here. I can't work with him.

MANNY: Why?

DIMITRI: Because I'm from Cyprus.

Pause

He's talking about being in the British army while Cyprus was a British colony. He's talking about the "terrorists" who would attack them. The terrorists *from Cyprus*. He's talking about those filthy bastards and their dirty fighting and how savage hot it was. Savage. And he's already asked me where I'm from.

MANNY: What did you tell him?

DIMITRI: I asked him why he thought it would help him to know.

Pause.

So. We have six days until the next session. I can gather my notes. I'm happy to liaise with whoever takes over...

MANNY: I don't see the problem.

DIMITRI: In what way do you not see the problem?

MANNY: In fact, what I see is the establishment of trust and the beginnings of an authentic bond in remarkable time. He opened up to you. Very quickly. He was effing and blinding a week ago. And now he's showing you his medals. Sharing personal history. And the improvement in the forms from one week to the next is –

DIMITRI: The fucking forms…

MANNY: It's four more sessions, Dimitri. Four more hours of your life. Four hours that could make a big difference to him. How many people has he had to start again with? You wanted to be different. And you've already shown him that. That is the healing. If you leave now, if he starts again with someone new, it would hit him at the very core –

DIMITRI: He asks me every session where I'm from. What's it going to do to his healing when he finds out? What's it going to do to the numbers? They're going to shoot up –

MANNY: That's not going to happen because he's not going to find out. There's no reason that within the next four hours of being with him he would need to know that information.

DIMITRI: He's bringing pictures next week. Of Cyprus –

MANNY: The medals and the pictures are lovely exercises in bonding. But as we established last week, these sessions are about the recent attack.

DIMITRI: Yes, but –

MANNY: Were the attackers Cypriot?

DIMITRI: No –

MANNY: Well then there wouldn't be any reason for him to talk about Cyprus any more. And you'll be so busy with the CBT that the question of your origin won't come up.

Look, this is how it goes. He spends the first couple of weeks sizing you up. Trying to place you. Figure out as much as he can about you. And then he forgets you and wants to talk about himself. That's the urge that drove him here in the first place. That's what he needs.

Pause.

DIMITRI: I can't do it.

Pause.

I can't. I'm sorry.

Silence.

MANNY: Ok.

Pause.

Fine. We'll find someone else.

Long silence.

DIMITRI: My grandfather lost his voice.

MANNY: I'll have a look and see who's available –

DIMITRI: He lost his voice because he hardly used it. My grandmother was such a force. She was the matriarch. You'd walk in and say "Hi Grandad, how are you?" And he'd open his mouth to answer and she would jump in and say "He's fine, he's fine. He just had his lunch. He was a bit constipated this morning but the lentils did the job." And he'd just close his mouth and sit back.

MANNY: Is that what reminded you –?

DIMITRI: He was one of eleven children. When he was twelve years old, his dad told him there were too many mouths to feed. He had to go and learn a trade. And they put him on a donkey and sent him out of the village to the town. And he became a cobbler's apprentice. When we were little he had a shoe shop.

He married my grandmother because she was even poorer than he was. She said, *he was short and ugly but he was the first to ask so what are you gonna do?* She was illiterate. He taught her how to read and write. He built them a house. With his own hands. Room by room. She would make the bricks out of mud and straw and bake them in the sun and he would come home from work and stack them up. And then they rented it to the British General's family and moved into the shed at the back. When my dad was a baby, in the winter the only place in the shed that wasn't freezing was the cupboard. So they kept him in the cupboard. Until it got warmer.

When my dad was a bit older there was an attack on the British base, and the British soldiers rounded as many locals up as they could and arrested them. Grandad was one of them. My dad saw him in the back of a truck. His hands above his head. His bike flung in the ditch. He ran all the way home, crying and found the army general in the house and the general drove to the camp and got them to free my grandfather. Vouched for him.

They got drunk on whisky that night. The two men.

It was a complicated dynamic…

Us and them.

Pause.

I was in the army. We all were.

SCENE SIX

FITZ: Where you from?

DIMITRI: I'm based in East London.

FITZ: No… Where you… *from* from? What's your… origin? Dimitri… Where's that name from?

DIMITRI: Is that important to you?

FITZ: What?

DIMITRI: To know where my name is from.

FITZ: Yeah.

DIMITRI: Why is it important?

FITZ: What, is it Russian?… It could be Eastern European, like.

Pause. **DIMITRI** *does not reply.*

FITZ: Narrow it down for me at least.

DIMITRI: It's my grandfather's name. I was named after my grandfather.

FITZ: …Who lived in…

Pause.

DIMITRI: Cyprus.

FITZ *lets this sink in. Nods his head.*

FITZ: I thought so. I thought so. I knew it. *(He pronounces his name in a Greek accent.) Dimitri. Yiasou Dimitri. Ti kaneis Dimitri? Kala? Kala.*

SCENE SEVEN

MANNY: The dreaded double From. Hard to outmanoeuvre.

DIMITRI: Yes. I'm still working on my evasion tactics. They're pretty limited.

Pause.

Do you… How do you… Have you ever…

MANNY: I find that if you're able to retain a certain mystery about your background it can be interesting… favourable even. People tend to project all sorts of things. Usually their own identity. Be it North African, Latin American, Spanish even. It's possible to travel most of the world and get local's rates just by maintaining a level of ethnic ambiguity.

DIMITRI: So there are some perks.

MANNY: Some.

Pause.

Indian. Tamil. Second generation. So, Acton, mostly.

How's city life compared to island life?

DIMITRI: There's something about the anonymity of this place that is… comforting. A relief. Back home I could go out for a couple of hours with friends, come back in time for dinner and my grandmother knew exactly where I'd been and who I'd been with. We called it the Greekvine. It was worse for the girls.

MANNY: Ah yes. We refer to it as The Desi Aunty Hotline.

DIMITRI: I miss… belonging, even though it came at a cost.

MANNY: There's always a price to pay, if you stay, if you go. It's all a negotiation.

DIMITRI: What did you find yourself negotiating?

MANNY: Me? Oh, well. Lots. Lots and lots over a lifetime… I could join the band, but only as a hobby. I could run my own business instead of the family's, but only if they had a say in what that business was… And how it was run. I can help a range of people, but only if the forms are filled. I was accepted into the friendship groups at school, but only if I could be both fully assimilated, and also their cool brown mate who gave them some street cred even though I wasn't actually that cool… Apart from playing the bass. I play bass. In the band. So.

Pause.

But yes. It is a constant negotiation. And you've paid a big price for leaving. It must have been lonely.

DIMITRI: It's a close-knit community. Everyone's related either through blood or marriage. But there was always this influence from outside. In some ways it made us close ranks even tighter.

SCENE EIGHT

FITZ: We got sent up to the villages, up in the mountains there. That's where they'd hide out. The terrorists. We all knew it. I was only seventeen. I almost pissed my pants there and then. I stood out like a sore thumb and all. I was the only black-skinned boy in the regiment. I was already sweating before we even left the camp. It was cooler up there though. Up in the mountains. First time we got some respite from that hellish sun o' yours. Jesus.

SCENE NINE

DIMITRI: My dad was walking home from school one day with his sister when a group of Indian soldiers drove up in a couple of jeeps. At least, that's what he called them. I think it was more likely they were Nepalese. Gurkhas maybe. They parked up by a field and jumped out. He hid behind his sister and watched these men, similar colouring to them, speaking a strange language, turbaned heads – they'd never seen anything like it. The men walked into the field, all the time discussing, debating, gesticulating. More children on their way home gathered near my dad and his sister to watch, my dad peering out from behind his sister, curiosity getting the better of him.

SCENE TEN

FITZ: So we walked round the narrow streets. Past the houses all cobbled together by hand. Everyone staring at us from their doorways. I'd nod and they'd nod back. And the higher we went, there was this smell. Sort of pungent. Earthy like. And it was so familiar. It drove me crazy. I kept trying to follow it, but Stan got pissed off, spat on the floor, so we called it a day. Went back.

SCENE ELEVEN

DIMITRI: They were coming to some kind of agreement. So they headed back to the jeeps, started unloading equipment, carrying it down to the middle of the field. Setting it up, hammering stakes into the ground, putting on protective gear. Limbering up. A couple of the braver kids ventured closer, trying to get their hands on some of the equipment, but the soldiers warned them back to the edge of the field. Finally, it seemed they were ready.

SCENE TWELVE

FITZ: On my day off I headed straight back up there. I'd been thinking about that smell. I went back to that village and followed my nose so to speak. It was like I was looking for home. And I finally got to this building. It was all crumbling. It didn't have a roof but the four walls were just about standing. And the smell was so strong. I didn't even think about what I was doing, I didn't stop to check it out, I just climbed right over and into it.

I landed on my arse and it took a minute to get over the pain and then I saw something move and I grabbed my gun and aimed and when I looked up it was a goat. A little one. There were loads of them. Baby ones with floppy ears all crying and jingling their bells. They were terrified of me. But then one of them comes forward slowly and the others get all brave and follow him and the next thing I know I've got goats all over me chewing on my clothes and trying to get in my pockets. And I sit there like a bloody moron. Just sitting there with the goats.

And I'm laughing cos it tickles and I'm swearing at these little blighters and I don't know how long I was there but I look up and there's this girl staring at me from the gate. I jump up and she makes a run for it and by the time I've straightened myself out and dusted myself off she's back with her dad and he's staring at me from the gate too. He looks at my uniform. The state of me. And then he opens the gate, jerks his head and says "*Ela. Ela.*" So I follow him out and we walk down the road and the girl's walking ahead shouting something at the house down the road, and we go through a gate and there's a sort of courtyard with a tree and some grapevines growing up like a sort of roof. This woman comes out with a big plate of food and dumps it on the table there and she looks up as we come in, and she stops when she sees me, just for a second, and then she says "*Kopiase.*" *Kopiase.*

(**DIMITRI** *recognises the word.*)

You can't translate that exactly can you? We don't have it in us do we. In English. It's not the same is it.

DIMITRI: It means welcome, come in. Sit down. Eat. It's a bit like the French *Bon apetit.*

FITZ: No. It's not.

So I sit down and eat with this family and that little girl is eyeing me the whole time. Doesn't take her eyes off me. And I'm thinking, *Fill your boots Fitz, my boy, because you're deep behind the enemy lines now and any moment you're done for so fill your fucking boots my son.* And the food's delicious. Some kind of stew. I hadn't had a proper home cooked meal for…

And then the coffee comes in those tiny little cups and I drink the whole thing up and my mouth gets filled with the dregs of it. I start choking on it and they all start laughing and the man there shows me I got to sip it halfway and then leave the muddy bit at the bottom.

And after a bit I get up and so does he. I don't know what to say. It's been bloody lovely and I think, *if I get a bullet to the back of my head now, so be it.* And he nods and I nod back and I look at the little girl and she's staring at me. And then I head back all relaxed and ready for Kingdom Come. But I make it all the way back to the camp and then Stan and all the rest are taking the mick out of the state of me.

Reckon I must have shacked up with one of the local girls. Had a bit of a fumble behind an olive tree. So I let them think it.

SCENE THIRTEEN

DIMITRI: The discussion dies down and they're in some kind of formation and one of them gives the order and they begin. Suddenly a soldier runs forward and lobs something with all his might out of his hand. Before the kids know what's happening, another of them responds by swinging a weapon of some kind and crack, it makes contact and the ball is flying to the far end of the field. Three of the men over that side start running in the direction of it and the other two start running up and down, from one end to the other. The fielders retrieve the ball and throw it back to the bowler. The kids are captivated. After a while they get the general gist and start cheering whenever a batter manages a few runs. In the break the soldiers beckon the kids over, start teaching them how to bowl, letting them have a go with the cricket bat.

That must have been the late forties. Just before India got its independence. And they were out there, bolstering the numbers of the British army, playing cricket in another colonised field.

SCENE FOURTEEN

FITZ: Every time I got a day off I'd go back. The mum there wouldn't even bat an eyelid. After a while she started babbling away at me like I was one of the rest. I didn't understand it really, but I picked up a few words. *Ela. Ate. Katse. Kopiase.* Third time I went I brought some tea bags and a bottle of whisky. He loved that. Old Andreas.

And one time the little girl got up after the food and led me back to the goats. Opened the gate and we sat there with the goats and I swear to god that smell.

And then about six months later we were all on patrol in the town down there. It was hot as hell as usual, and we got to the square with the fountain and started jostling for the water and the girl, I think it was her, she walked past with bags full of shopping. I looked up as she passed by and then she dropped something. It was a lemon. So

I rushed over to pick it up and just as I opened my mouth to call her back I got shoved to the floor and there was ringing in my ears and I didn't know which way was up and something slapped me on the back of the head and it was an arm. A fucking arm. Just an arm. On its own. And I'm trying to get up but there's stone and brick flying about and dust everywhere and where the fountain was there's just a hole. And where Stan was there's. There's bits of flesh all over the place. I can't hear a thing. I think I'm shouting. I think I'm up, stumbling about, trying to save someone, but there's no one to save. There's no one left. Just bits and pieces. And a hole. And I'm holding the arm, cradling it like. And trying to look for the other pieces, trying to put him back together. And finally the others arrive and they bundle me in the ambulance and take me back. There's not a scratch on me. Just my eardrum burst.

Every night. For nigh on sixty year. I'm back there holding that arm looking into that hole. Trying to shout. Every night.

Long pause.

Oh, I got you something.

FITZ *reaches into his pocket and pulls out a lemon. He throws it to* **DIMITRI** *who catches it.*

Be lucky.

END OF ACT ONE.

Act Two

SCENE ONE

DIMITRI: Are you angry?

MANNY: Why do you think I would be angry?

DIMITRI: Well, for obvious… It's obvious. I…

MANNY: Who would I be angry with?

DIMITRI: Me.

MANNY: Do you want me to be angry?

DIMITRI: Ok. Look. Can we just. Stop.

MANNY: Stop…?

DIMITRI: With the…

MANNY: The…session?

DIMITRI: No, not with the session. Just with the… technique…

MANNY: What would be helpful?

DIMITRI: I want to know how you… There must be some… feelings about what I just told you and I… want to know.

MANNY: Shall we maybe start with your feelings about what you just told me?

DIMITRI: Ok. Well I'm still in shock. It was a lot to hear… I'm scared. That you're angry. That I'm out of my… But I also stand by it. He asked. And I told him. He'd figured it out anyway. And then it happened. He was telling me and telling me.

MANNY: He described an extremely violent episode in your country's history.

DIMITRI: It felt so loaded. In that room. As soon as he knew where I was from. I could tell he was itching with it. Like he'd been holding it in for years, decades, and finally he'd found the right person. There was no need for explanation or context. He knew I knew. I'd be able to picture the place, the people, I'd understand. That's the irony. We were on opposite sides. What *they* did to *us* was… But he was there, in my country. We were both there – at different times, but we were there. So we get it in a way no one else can. And that's why… it felt like… we were put in that room for exactly that.

MANNY: You sound very clear.

DIMITRI: But…?

MANNY: No buts. Honestly. It sounds like your instinct is telling you that whatever this process is, it's happening in the way it needs to happen.

DIMITRI: Ok.

MANNY: Also, you were in the room. You experienced it.

DIMITRI: I did. But I'm also learning. I'm going through a process. I haven't finished learning yet and so…

MANNY: What are you doubting.

DIMITRI: I don't doubt it exactly but, if I'm being devil's advocate –

MANNY: –If you're looking at this from another angle.

DIMITRI: –Yes, then, well, if it is my instinct that's telling me this was so right, can I trust it?

MANNY: Good question. Certainly a lot of what we do is to give you enough experience, and a training so thorough, that you're able to trust your instincts and make the right choices in the moment with each individual.

DIMITRI: Yes, but then I'm still in that process. So at what point in the training does my instinct become a thing I can trust?

MANNY: Well, that's impossible to… But maybe what is helpful is to ask, what's another way of looking at this? On the one hand there is a strong sense of it being the right thing to have happened. A sense of fate, perhaps. But, what else?

DIMITRI: Maybe I'm way too close. Maybe I can't see this objectively at all. Maybe this is a horrible mix of naivety and rookie over-confidence and personal shit and ego that I think is creating this wonderful journey to Redemption, when really it's just a shit-storm in a chipped mug.

MANNY: A very different view.

DIMITRI: Is that how you see it?

MANNY: I'm thinking about my own contribution to this… recipe… and what would be best for everyone going forward.

Pause.

DIMITRI: I fucked up your forms. You're definitely pissed off about that.

MANNY: What do you understand to be the point of those forms?

DIMITRI: It's part of working in an institution. A way of keeping track of a client's progress.

MANNY: You did once refer to them as The Fucking Forms.

DIMITRI: I do have some issues with the forms. They seem like a crude way of assessing a human being's journey. Mine certainly hasn't been linear.

MANNY: No. Of course. They are, ironically, in part borne out of a more person-centred approach. An immediate source of feedback from the service user. They are also a crude way of assessing a human being's journey. And they're also strongly tied to our funding. We need a certain percentage of "wins" each year to justify the amount of patients we're able to support. That's why my approach to them was perhaps a bit… loaded.

DIMITRI: Did you ever think about just running this place for private clients? Surely that would be so much easier. And more lucrative. Cut out the forms, the system…

MANNY: That's certainly what I was encouraged to do…

DIMITRI: By who? Family?

MANNY: Yes.

DIMITRI: So why didn't you?

MANNY: I guess I just love a well filled out form too much.

Pause.

The biggest concern here is that a process has been started that isn't likely to come to any kind of closure in the few sessions left. Facing and working through trauma, especially trauma that's been suppressed for decades is a complicated process that needs time. We have a duty of care that includes making sure our clients don't leave us even worse off. It's not just the forms that get fucked up Dimitri, it's the client.

Pause.

One option is to see if we can get him some more sessions. In exceptional cases you can make the argument that an allocation of six more sessions is important.

DIMITRI: This is an exceptional case. PTSD, especially in veterans, is surely the most textbook –

MANNY: You'd think. We'll need to check with him first of course, and then we'll need to make a strong case as to why this individual will delay another person from getting their six sessions because it's in his interest and everyone else's that he receive it.

DIMITRI: And everyone else's?

MANNY: Yes.

Pause.

You did mention in your notes that there was a threat of retaliation.

DIMITRI: Retaliation?

MANNY: Early in the sessions he seemed to be adamant that he would take revenge on those who'd attacked him.

DIMITRI: He's eighty-two. He can barely get up out of his chair. It was bravado. You said it yourself. Sizing me up, swearing.

MANNY: Of course. And. It's a way of having a stronger case for getting him some more time.

DIMITRI: Right. I see. So what he's been through. What he's done for this country. Being a human in need isn't enough. We have to make him out to be a risk to himself and others.

MANNY: We're using your notes which are a direct record of his words to help him get more support. The support he deserves and that we have a duty to provide.

Pause.

And what about you?

DIMITRI: Me? Well, you can put in your notes that I'm not planning any form of retaliation.

MANNY: Are you sure?

DIMITRI: Pretty sure.

SCENE TWO

FITZ: You must have served then. If you're from Cyprus. You must have done your mandatory, what is it, a year, coupla years? What do they make you do?

DIMITRI: Mandatory conscription in Cyprus is two years.

FITZ: Good lad. Good. They need to bring that back in here. That would sort this country out. Coupla years National Service... Sort the whole country out that would.

I was in the park the other day. First thing. I always get out first thing. Rain or shine. Get a bit of fresh air in them lungs. That's why I'm still fighting fit son. Routine, like... And I'm sitting on this bench watching this fella in his uniform, boots, beret, the lot, shouting at these people. Yelling at them to drop and give him twenty, making them run around a tree, shoving their faces in the mud. And the lasses have got all this... bright coloured... exercise gear, lads with their pristine new shoes, hundred quid haircuts, being yelled at, sworn at... And then it's all over and everyone stands up and claps. They all clap. And then they're getting their phones out and he's talking about payment and see you tomorrow morning and then they all head off and he picks up his bag, looks back at the tree and wanders off too.

I worked twenty years doing night shift security when I left the army. Do you know what they pay you? And now these low ranking Jacks are making a mint telling businessmen to fuck off every other morning. They're raking it in. I could do that. You could do that. Ridiculous.

DIMITRI: It's an interesting evolution in military training.

FITZ: It's the world gone loopy, that's what it is.

DIMITRI: How are you feeling after last week's session? You shared a lot of very personal stuff. Maybe some things you haven't talked about for a long time.

FITZ: It was hard, like. Going back there. Remembering. But it was good. To talk about it.

DIMITRI: The flashbacks. Have they changed at all? Decreased maybe?

FITZ: Yeah, yeah. It's better.

DIMITRI: In what way.

FITZ: It's just got better, hasn't it. Like I don't think about it so much.

DIMITRI: You said that the flashbacks were happening every day. That they had been affecting you for a long time.

FITZ: Yeah, that's changed now. Like I said.

DIMITRI: Ok. Well that's great. I'm glad to hear that.

Pause.

It may be, Fitz, that things feel worse before they get better. Sometimes when we start to look at things from the past we might feel some relief, and we might also remember more things, or feel things we weren't able to feel before. That's also normal.

FITZ: Nah, it's good, like. I feel... good.

DIMITRI: Ok. Well, if you remember we started off talking about the attack that happened recently outside your home. And now we've moved on to talk about things that happened a long time ago. It might take longer to work through that. I wanted to check what you think about us requesting some more sessions together?

FITZ: More of these? With you?

DIMITRI: Yes. If you like.

FITZ: Talking?

DIMITRI: Yes.

FITZ: About what?

DIMITRI: Whatever you want to talk about, Fitz.

FITZ: Do I have to do that mindfulness stuff again?

DIMITRI: Only if you think it would help.

FITZ: And I can talk about the other stuff now?

DIMITRI: Yes. You can.

FITZ: Alright. Go on then. It's better than a poke in the eye.

DIMITRI: Ok.

FITZ: On one condition though. You do all them forms. I'm not doing any more of them forms.

DIMITRI: Ah, well, the thing is, we have to fill in a special form to explain why we're asking for more time together. I've got it here. I thought we could take a look.

FITZ: You know what to put. Just say I'm a veteran. I've got shell shock.

DIMTRI: We prefer the term PTSD.

FITZ: Exactly. Put that down. See? I'll only mess it up.

DIMITRI: I also wanted to check with you… The thing is… it would help our case if I was able to say that I am also… concerned that you might be thinking of harming those who had attacked you. Those young men, outside your home.

Pause.

FITZ: I'm gonna kick seven shades of shit out of them. Put that down on the fucking form.

DIMITRI: Are you sure? Because I –

FITZ: Put it down.

DIMITRI: Ok. Ok.

SCENE THREE

MANNY: He asked you directly if you had served.

DIMITRI: Yes.

MANNY: And?

DIMITRI: I told him what he already knew.

When Britain finally left, we had fourteen years of independence. Precious years. A whole island united and free, finally. But then in 1974 it all changed. Again. First Greece took over. Then Turkey invaded. My father was caught up in it all. He disappeared for twenty-four terrifying hours. And then he came home. Safe, uninjured, and angry.

I was conceived soon after. And like every male of my generation I had to do National Service. I was a pretty active kid. I held the records for athletics in my school. Played for the football and basketball team. My best friend was this chubby kid called Socrates. We called him Sock for short. We went in together. The first month was hell for him. They called him a mama's boy, did impressions of him, singled him out for extra work, punishments, when he could barely do the regular stuff. I couldn't stand it. But he just kept cracking those jokes. He kept giving as good as he got. He never once gave in, even when his face was in the dirt, glasses cracked. He kept swearing right back at them, insulting their mothers. And he won them over in the end.

They could see I found the physical stuff easy. So they started giving me the long shifts in the midday sun. Just standing there, sweating. You start to hallucinate after a while. Mad dogs and Englishmen... And then my sergeant came and relieved me. Chucked me a coin as he was walking away and told me to clean the latrines. I had to scrape the shit off the walls of the toilet. With a coin. They woke me up every morning with a punch to the balls. Character building apparently. But you know the worst bit? The thing that broke me? It was taking orders from someone so much stupider than me.

MANNY: Is that how you see Fitz?

DIMITRI: No. No. I've got so much respect for Fitz. I'm not talking about education. My own grandfather… In England everything is about class. The route you take in the army is based on class. In Cyprus it's all about the *meson*. Who you know. Who your family know. That's what determines things. I didn't know the right people. But more than that. This whole breaking down of you, turning you into a machine that just takes orders, it doesn't work when you're only there for a couple of years. I had to go back out into the world and think for myself. I didn't give a shit about all that stuff. Teach me how to use a gun and if those fuckers invade us again I'll be in the front line with the best of them. But don't mess with me till I don't even recognise myself.

Some of us hardened up. Played the game. Some of us got the gist of handling a gun and pointed it at our own face.

I got out. And came here. But it meant I could never go back.

SCENE FOUR

FITZ: You ever go back there? Back home?

DIMITRI: I haven't been for a while.

FITZ: Must have changed a bit. I hear it's all big hotels and nightclubs now. One of the nurses who does the home visit. She was going on about her holiday over there. Said they danced all night every night, to English music, by an English DJ, surrounded by English people. And then got on the plane, came back to England.

DIMITRI: Yes, that sounds like Ayia Napa.

FITZ: That's the one. We never went up there. Sounds a bit much for me. I was never much of a dancer. Two left feet, me. Just about managed the left right left right.

DIMITRI: What's the nurse's name?

FITZ: That one's Mellinda. Lovely lady. Always makes us a cup of tea. Doesn't rush me. Always up for a bit of a natter. If it's not Mellinda there's Gloria. She's alright and all. Cheeky lass. Won't let me get away with anything. Tells me off sometimes. Just like my…

DIMITRI: Like who?

FITZ: My mum. She was very strict she was. I couldn't get away with anything. Eyes in the back of her head that one. That's why I joined the army. To get a bit of a breather… Nah… It was tough in them days. She had to keep us in hand. Boys running around getting into all sorts of trouble. Some our fault. Some not… She had her hands full that's for sure.

DIMITRI: So you have siblings?

FITZ: Had. I'm the last one standing.

DIMITRI: That must be tough. Lonely.

FITZ: There's the ones next door. They're the ones who found me the day those little shits gave me a hiding. He helped me back up, half carried me to their flat. And the Mrs saw to me while he called the police. Polish fella. Checked in on me the next day and all.

DIMITRI: I'm glad to hear that, Fitz. It sounds like they care about you.

FITZ: You got brothers? Sisters?

A knock at the door.

DIMITRI: Sorry about that. No one should be… The room is booked for us so there shouldn't be any interruptions.

Another bolder knock.

You were telling me about your mother.

MANNY's *voice arguing with someone.*

FITZ: What's all that?

DIMITRI: I'm not sure… but I think it's being handled so –

The door opens.

*An **OFFICER** in a uniform that is not quite police, not quite military, strides in, followed by **MANNY**.*

MANNY: You do not have the authority to do this –

OFFICER: Fitzroy John Williams? Are you Mr Williams?

DIMITRI: *(Standing.)* Hey, hey you can't come in here.

MANNY: I'm going to have to insist that you –

OFFICER: *(To **DIMITRI**.)* If you could just. *(To **FITZ**.)* Are you Fitzroy John Williams.

DIMITRI: Who are you?

MANNY: All questions should be addressed to me. Let's step outside and –

OFFICER: I'm going to have to ask you to take a step back while I speak to Mr Williams here.

FITZ: *(Struggling out of his seat.)* What's going on?

OFFICER: Are you Fitzroy John Williams?

DIMITRI: *(To **FITZ**.)* You don't have to answer that.

FITZ: Who wants to know?

OFFICER: UK Border Agency, Immigration Enforcement. Do you have any I.D on your person?

MANNY: If you don't step outside of this room now I will call the authorities.

OFFICER: I am the authorities. *(To **FITZ**.)* Your identification please.

DIMITRI: He doesn't have to show you anything.

FITZ: What's going on? What's this all about?

OFFICER: Mr Williams, I'm going to need to see that I.D.

FITZ: What do you mean Immigration?

OFFICER: Immigration Enforcement and Future Borders.

DIMITRI: What? That's enough. You have no right –

OFFICER: You must be Dimitri Poli- Poli-carpou. I will be happy to discuss your concerns once I have finished with Mr Williams here. Mr Williams, it has come to our attention that your paperwork is not in order and that you are missing some documents that jeopardise your right to remain in this country.

FITZ: What you talking about?

DIMITRI: This is absolutely unacceptable. Manny –

OFFICER: I am here to issue you with this letter. *(He holds out an envelope to* **FITZ***.)*

FITZ: *(Looking at the envelope in the* **OFFICER***'s hand.)* What's that?

OFFICER: It's from the Home Office Mr Williams, informing you that your right to remain in this country has been forfeited and that you must report to the Home Office immediately to begin the process of your removal from the UK.

FITZ: I'm not taking that. That's not for me.

DIMITRI: I'm calling the police. I don't know who you are but you have no right to speak to my client or hand him any document. This is a private space.

OFFICER: *(Lowering his hand still holding the letter.)* Dimitri Policarpou is that correct?

DIMITRI: My name is of no concern to –

OFFICER: I want to thank you and Mr Tharma… kumar here for bringing Mr Williams to our attention.

MANNY: In what way is my name implicated in all –

OFFICER: Your report on Mr Williams' recent state of mind and your concern for the threat he poses to other civilians flagged him up on the system and from there we were able to –

FITZ: What you on about? What report?

DIMITRI: What do you mean? Report? *(To* **MANNY***.)* What did you do?

MANNY: Nothing. I haven't in any way disclosed any private… I have nothing to do with this.

OFFICER: An application was submitted on the twenty-first of this month requesting extra resources for Mr Williams. Among the details included were the dates, times and locations of these… meetings, and concerns about his violent behaviour.

MANNY: The form. The request. For more time…

DIMITRI: The form? The fucking form? Are you kidding me? They can use that to – to –

FITZ: What the hell is going on?

OFFICER: Mr Williams, you have overstayed your entitlement to be in this country. You are here illegally and –

FITZ: How dare you –

OFFICER: –AND I am here to offer you the chance to leave the United Kingdom voluntarily in order to avoid your forcible return.

FITZ: Return? Where do you want me to go?

OFFICER: This is a one-time offer to have your travel expenses back to Jamaica paid for by the –

FITZ: Jamaica?! What you on about?

OFFICER: Isn't that your country of origin?

FITZ: I'm British. I'm a British citizen.

OFFICER: That is not correct, I'm afraid.

FITZ: Yes it bloody well is.

OFFICER: You weren't born here.

FITZ: Doesn't matter. I was born as, and have always been, a British Citizen.

OFFICER: What you were was a British Subject until 1962 I believe when Jamaica gained independence and from that –

FITZ: Don't you dare tell me my own history.

DIMITRI: Please, Fitz, it's ok. There is no way they can use confidential client information to trick people into –

OFFICER: We are empowered to use any source of information to tackle immigration offences and support the safe removal of illegal migrants from the UK. And as part of my remit I will be checking all paperwork pertaining to yourselves, your business and any other persons of concern connected to it.

DIMITRI: Don't threaten me –

MANNY: My documents and the documents pertaining to this organisation are in perfect order, I assure you –

OFFICER: It will also be noted whether you chose to co-operate with this process today or whether you decided to obstruct a government officer from removing an illegal –

DIMITRI: He's an elderly man for god's sake –

MANNY: Ok well let's just. First of all you do of course have our – my – full co-operation if –

DIMITRI: What?

MANNY: – IF this is indeed a matter of legal process –

DIMITRI: What are you saying?

MANNY: – This organisation prides itself on being scrupulous in its… in every way –

DIMITRI: Manny, no.

MANNY: – and we will of course co-operate fully with any legal process… But this is extremely heavy handed and quite an exceptional way of conducting an investigation into someone who is… who is not really a threat to anyone…

OFFICER: That remains to be ascertained.

FITZ: *(To* **MANNY**.*)* Where you from?

MANNY: I beg your pardon?

FITZ: You heard me. Where you from. Where are your people from?

MANNY: I don't know what that has to do with… I'm from Acton.

FITZ: Nah. Nah… You're from tiger people in't ya. You got tiger blood in you, you have. I can tell. I can always tell. Tigers. That's what your people are.

DIMITRI: Fitz, It's ok. I know this must have come as a shock –

MANNY: He's talking about my Tamil background. Isn't that right? The tiger reference? I'm afraid it's more spreadsheets and form filling these days than militant action…

OFFICER: Tamil? Isn't that a terrorist organisation?

MANNY: No. It's an ethnic group. Of people.

OFFICER: I'll have to look into that.

DIMITRI: So now we're being investigated too?

OFFICER: These are exceptional times. Laws and policies have changed. The heightened risk to this country from foreign threat means that we now have the right to –

FITZ: What do you know about that? Eh? What the hell do you know about that? Foreign threat? You haven't got clue. You think I'm the threat? Me?

OFFICER: It's my duty to keep our borders secure and I will –

FITZ: Tell me something. You military?

OFFICER: I am a Defender of Future Borders –

FITZ: Defender of…? Have you ever served in the military.

OFFICER: That is not –

FITZ: Answer me boy!

OFFICER: Yes I have.

FITZ: Ok then. What rank are you.

OFFICER: I am an officer –

FITZ: An officer?

OFFICER: No, an Immigration Enforcement Officer–

FITZ: What is your rank son?

OFFICER: Corporal.

FITZ: Corporal?

OFFICER: Lance. Corporal.

FITZ: Lance Corporal. And have you ever been in active combat.

OFFICER: No.

FITZ: Have you ever come under fire. Returned fire.

OFFICER: I have not.

FITZ: Have you ever been posted to the very heart of it. Ran towards it. Looked it in the eye, on its own turf. This foreign threat.

OFFICER: I don't know what this has to do with –

FITZ: Have you done that Lance Corporal?

OFFICER: I have not.

FITZ: No. Course not. That's why you think an eighty-two-year-old-man is the enemy. I come here because they came over and got me. They came over and asked us to help. Me. My mum. All of us. Common Citizenship, Common Cause. That's what they told us. They already paid my ticket: To come over here. I fought for Queen and country. Seen my men blown into nothing to keep this place safe. Good people. Fighting the real enemy. All that was left of them was a scrap of flesh they couldn't even send home to be buried. And that scrap is still worth fifty of the likes of you. And you come in here and tell me thank you very much old boy but you're not one of us anymore? How dare you. You want my I.D? Here's my bloody I.D.

Shakily, he pulls out the picture of him as a soldier. Holds it up.

There it is. Go on. Take a look. See that uniform? Count the stripes.

OFFICER: I'm afraid that is not an acceptable form of –

FITZ: Count the fucking stripes son and then call me an illegal again. I dare you.

Pause.

OFFICER: Well, sergeant. Unfortunately my orders still stand. You can walk out now, with your dignity and your stripes intact. That's my offer.

FITZ: Or else?

OFFICER: Or else you will be forcibly removed, and Mr Tharmakumar here will need to facilitate your removal from his premises. We can help you pack, arrange your flight and get this all over with quickly and quietly. Then you can appeal if you have grounds to do so. Deport first, appeal later.

FITZ: I'm not going anywhere with you. This isn't right. It's a mistake.

OFFICER: Well if that's your final word on it. Mr Tharmakumar?

Pause. They turn to **MANNY**.

MANNY: *(Avoiding eye contact.)* I'm sorry. But I'm going to have to ask you to leave the premises.

DIMITRI: Manny, no.

FITZ *lets it sink in and then nods. Begins to move.*

MANNY: Not you, Mr Williams.

FITZ *stops. They all look at* **MANNY**.

MANNY *looks at the* **OFFICER**.

You failed to show me any form of official identification. I've seen no warrant or any paperwork confirming your right to enter these premises and indeed this room. You may well have been given the authority to investigate Mr Williams' status, but in this moment he is our client and under our care and he will stay here.

The **OFFICER** *takes this in.*

OFFICER: *(Places the letter on the chair. To* **FITZ**.*)* You're not meant to be here. You had your chance. Now you'll be leaving in handcuffs.

The **OFFICER** *walks out.* **MANNY** *deflates for a moment, the front he put on now dissipated. He looks at* **FITZ**, *then* **DIMITRI**, *then he walks out.* **FITZ** *shakily lowers himself back into his chair.*

FITZ: *(Shaken, disturbed.)* He shouldn't speak to me like that... It's not right... I've got a letter from the Queen... He should – he should speak to Major... Colonel Anderson... He knows me. If he was alive he'd vouch for me, he would... I got... medals... I got...

DIMITRI: It's ok, Fitz. You don't have to –

FITZ: I'm sorry. I'm sorry. I'm so sorry.

DIMITRI: What? No. Fitz, you've got nothing to be sorry for.

FITZ: I am. I am. I'm sorry. I...

SCENE FIVE

DIMITRI *and* **FITZ** *sit in the room as usual. The mood is heavy, haunted. A long silence.*

DIMITRI: What we have managed to do is get you another session here with me to make up for... last week. And then hopefully as the case is resolved we can add more hours.

Pause.

We've written a formal letter both to the head of our department and also to the Home Office clarifying our position regarding your notes and issuing a complaint about the way they were misused... misinterpreted...

Pause.

I understand you have someone who is supporting you legally? How is that going?

Fitz?

FITZ: Yeah?

DIMITRI: How's it going?

FITZ: They said I had a strong... a strong case. Said my record of service... service to the... said it would make a strong case.

Government tried to make out there weren't any records… Said I'm not on the system… It don't make sense… It was cos of what they found on the system that started this trouble wasn't it?… But then they're saying there's no record of me on the… But the lawyer said that wasn't possible. He's getting all my records… all my files… Got a reporter over too. She interviewed me about it all. Said there were a few of us. In the same boat, like. She's doing an article with all of us in. For the newspaper.

DIMITRI: Have you been able to rest? Eat?

FITZ *looks at him.*

No. I imagine not.

Pause.

FITZ: It's not… I ain't been there since I was a kid. This is my home. I'm sure it's lovely and all that but… it's not my home. I don't know anyone… I haven't got a clue… I don't care what it says on the papers. I know it. Inside. Through and through. British.

Would you… could you ever go back?

DIMITRI: To Cyprus? To live? Well, the truth is I can't. I'm not allowed.

FITZ: You're not allowed to go back. I'm not allowed to stay.

DIMITRI: Yes… It's… I'm so sorry, Fitz. I never thought for a minute it was possible for them to… I will of course help in any way I can. If there are documents that need reading or filling out you could bring them with you. I could…

FITZ: Don't. You shouldn't. I don't want you to.

DIMITRI: It's the very least we can do. And I personally –

FITZ: I mean it. It's not right –

DIMITRI: This is an exceptional situation, Fitz. And I –

FITZ: We went back. Back up there. After… After they… the attack. We went back up there and rounded everyone up. Anyone we could find. Took 'em away in a truck. And then we torched the place. All of it. It went up like kindling. The heat and the dry and the straw and wood.

Like kindling. I stormed through there myself. Shouting. Shooting. The house was already on fire. I stopped for a second. Watched it burn. Then I headed to the other place. I didn't see her, but I knew she'd be hiding in there. I fired a round first. Heard the animals squealing. Then I set it alight myself. Watched it go up. Listened to the screams. No idea if it was man or beast. Or girl. Torched it all.

Pause.

DIMITRI: Is that what's been keeping you from sleeping?

FITZ: I was a machine. A machine. And for what?

Pause.

I appreciate all that you... But it's probably best if... Hand over them forms, son. I'll do the last one meself.

Pause.

DIMITRI: *(Brings out the form. Hesitates. Holds on to it.)* I am angry. I am very angry right now. And that's how *I* know I'm not a machine. I also know that a machine doesn't spend years and years unable to sleep because of what he saw and did. I know a machine doesn't feel fear and loneliness and regret and shame.

I haven't been back for almost twenty years. I haven't spoken to my father in that time. There is a line that passes right through Cyprus now. A scar. Separating the North from the South. Us and them. Still. Now. And the longer it goes on, the harder it is to imagine anything else.

There is a lot out there that neither of us have much power over. But there is a small frontier here, in this room.

What if it stops here? What if we decide it stops? What if we draw a line under it all? Today. In this room.

Pause.

FITZ: You mean that?

Ok. Ok then.

As long as it doesn't mean another bloody form.

DIMITRI: No more forms. I promise.

He goes to put the forms away.

FITZ: No no. Hand it over. I don't want your tiger boss getting his knickers in a twist.

DIMITRI: I don't think it's appropriate to refer to him –

FITZ: I know, I know. You can't say anything nowadays. Just hand it over.

DIMITRI: Are you sure? I could read it out if you –

FITZ: Nah, you're alright. *(Produces his glasses.)* I brought me glasses this time.

FITZ puts on his glasses and proceeds to fill in the form. He glances up at DIMITRI who is staring at him.

What?

DIMITRI: I thought… I wasn't sure if… you were able to…

FITZ: What, read? What do you think I am? I forgot me bleedin' glasses! That's all.

DIMITRI: Of course. Of course.

FITZ hands him the form. They stand.

DIMITRI: Thank you. And see you next week.

FITZ: *(Struggling to express himself. Decides on something simple.)* Be lucky, yeah?

SCENE SIX

DIMITRI enters the room, switching on the light. He begins to prepare the room, placing the chairs, the clock, the tissues.

He checks his watch and looks out of the door.

No one there.

He sits in his chair and patiently waits.

Silence.

After a while he checks outside again.

Still no one.

He sits back in his chair. Waits.

More silence.

MANNY *walks by, sees the door ajar. Glances in and sees* **DIMITRI** *who looks up expecting* **FITZ**. *A moment of recognition between them.* **MANNY** *steps into the room and stands by the door respectfully.*

They both wait.

And wait.

Lights slowly fade.

END.

Acknowledgements

I am so grateful to the Criterion New Writers run by Greg Mosse, who first gave me the space, time and guidance to begin writing this play. To Ellandar Productions and Rogue Playwrights run by Iskandar R.Sharazuddin, for the chance to have a reading of an early extract of the play. To all those who read and gave thoughts and notes, thank you for helping me hone this. To Neil and the Finborough team, winning the ETPEP Award means so much.

I am also grateful to the many people who were affected by the Windrush Scandal – many of whom have yet to receive any compensation or justice – who spoke out and shared their stories. And a big thank you to those in Cyprus who shared our family stories – Koulla Sagredou, Pambos Economides, to Lex and Kay Economides for being my Cyprus home... and to my cousin Andreas Economides for sharing so much – thank you.

The ETPEP Award

The ETPEP Award is a playwriting prize for new UK playwrights who work or have worked in the theatre industry, run by the Finborough Theatre in association with the Experienced Theatre Practitioners Early Playwriting Trust (**ETPEP**).

The Award's purpose is to find and nurture a playwright who has worked in theatre for two years or more, either now or in the past, who is looking to further their ambitions and skill in the art and craft of playwriting. The award is not open to those who have previously had a play professionally produced, or who have worked in a literary department setting or as a paid script reader.

We look for a play of substance which contributes in some way to our understanding of the human condition or experience, from a writer with potential to enhance our political and social awareness.

The award is judged completely anonymously until the very final shortlist and interview stage, and brief feedback is provided on every entry.

Nina Millns, the 2021 winner, received a prize of £6,000, a development relationship with the Finborough Theatre including one-to-one dramaturgy with Finborough Theatre Artistic Director and playwright Neil McPherson; a staged reading performance of the winning play at the Finborough Theatre, London; and publication by Salamander Street, independent publisher of theatre, performance and live art.

The judges for the 2021 Award were Artistic Director of the Finborough Theatre and playwright Neil McPherson; Literary Manager of the Finborough Theatre and playwright Sue Healy; actor Oliver Ford Davies; actor, playwright and activist Athena Stevens; and Clive Webster of the Experienced Theatre Practitioners Early Playwriting Trust, which founded the award.

The 2022 award closes on 30 April 2022.

www.etpepaward.co.uk

www.finboroughtheatre.co.uk